# Hell Shall Not Prevail

**John Honeycutt**

**Copyright © 1997**

ISBN 1-57502-579-5

To correspond with Tony Honeycutt or for additional
copies of **"Hell Shall Not Prevail"** contact:
HICO Baptist Church
Post Office Box 934
Graham, NC 27253
(910) 376-6311

Printed in the USA by

**MORRIS PUBLISHING**
3212 East Highway 30 • Kearney, NE 68847 • 1-800-650-7888

# DEDICATIONS

To my wife and children who love God
and co-labor with me.

To my mother and grandmother
who taught me to be strong.

To Dr. E.T. Isely, my spiritual father.

To Dr. Frank McGuire, my spiritual teacher.

To Rev. Denny Wall, my beloved Pastor.

To all our faithful supporters.

# TABLE OF CONTENTS

# FOREWORD

*"Also, that the soul be without*

*knowledge, it is not good; and he that hasteth*

*with his feet sinneth."*

Proverbs 19:2

The intention of this book is to reveal the life and the work of the missionary. Many people have an understanding of missions, but little knowledge of the foreign missionary himself, particularly the third world missionary. They envision the missionary hacking his way through the bush, machete in one hand, Bible in the other hand, sweat rolling down his face, as he desperately spends the last of his energy to reach some long forgotten tribe. Upon reaching these people with bones in their noses, who are jumping up and down like a swarm of crazed grasshoppers, he stands before them and fearlessly opens his Bible to John 3:16. His eyes fixed, he begins to preach. After hearing this incredibly good news, a jungle revival breaks out. One by one each of these "bone-

1

nosed" people come to receive Christ. Without question or hesitation they discard their old beliefs. They bring out all the relics of their false religions and burn them before the man of God. The former witch doctor becomes the Pastor and a church is immediately erected. The brave missionary, his work now accomplished, begins to hack his way back into the thick and dark bush, searching for yet another long lost tribe.

Admittedly this picture is over dramatized. But, unfortunately this is the only picture most can envision. It appears the missionary has no needs, except his Bible and that trusty machete. His family does not exist, or if they do exist it is in some other world, where all of their needs are automatically being provided for without him. He has no decisions to make and no needs to provide for. His only purpose is to go forth. He is a spiritual "superman" immune to the needs of the world such as housing, food, clothing, comfort, and education for the kids.

It is true, missionaries are special. God has called them to evangelize across cultural and national boundaries. This in itself will provide for the many interesting stories we hear of different lands far away. But, still we must understand that they are not immune to the usual struggles of life. They have fears, frustrations, and goals. They make mistakes, they have dreams, they support families, and they live much like everyone else. Yet, to most people there is still a mystery about them.

What is it that is so strange about the missionary? Is he crazy? Is he super spiritual? What is needed is to unveil this mystery surrounding the missionary and his work. Unveiling this mystery is necessary for two reasons. First, Christians need a knowledge of the missionary's needs and work in order to pray and support him with an understanding heart. Second, many young people and others who are preparing to become missionaries need an accurate and straightforward report of missionary life. In many Bible schools, missionary candidates get the philosophy of missions,, but go to the field without any real idea of what life will be like. They need this information!

The intent of this book is to help people understand the life and work of the missionary. It will not and cannot tell you everything about missionaries, but is my prayer that by telling my story as a missionary and the story of the planting and growth of Karibuni Baptist Church in Kenya, East Africa, you might gain more insight into the world of missionaries. God bless you as you read!

# CHAPTER ONE

## - The Departure -

*"I am now ready to be offered, and the time*

*of my departure is at hand..."*

11 Tim. 4:6

*"Notwithstanding the Lord stood with me and*

*strengthened me; that by me the preaching*

*might be fully known..."*

11 Tim. 4:7

The day had finally arrived for our departure to Kenya, a small third world country off the coast of East Africa. My wife, my children, and I had anticipated this day for almost four years. I couldn't believe that we were really going. I had tickets, our bags were packed, but would we really go? Should we really go? Should I be doing this? As these questions raced through my mind like cars on a busy highway, my oldest daughter entered the room. I looked at her long golden hair, big beautiful blue eyes, and loving smile and wondered if I should be taking her away from all she knows? How will she feel towards me? These and many other questions continued to run through my mind. What about my mother, grandmother, and family left in America? What if something happens to them? I knew this was God's will but why couldn't I stop these questions from racing through my mind?

On the day of our departure our families planned a going away party for us. We would attend this party and afterwards load ourselves onto our church's van for the six-hour trip to Dulles International Airport in Washington, DC. At the going away party, the atmosphere was doleful. Everyone was walking around, but no one knew what to say. The strain of not seeing us again for at least two years was unyielding. I glanced around the room at our family members. As I scanned their faces I could see by their half-frowning, half-smiling expressions that they had mixed emotions just as I did. I looked at Tammy (my wife), then at her mother and father, and realized that for the first time in their lives they would soon be physically separated. I realized that Tammy would miss the Saturday morning shopping sprees with her mother, the walks in the park, and the quiet evenings spent sharing with her father. As I beheld my mother's tear-filled eyes, I felt particularly uneasy. We had live  with her while on deputation to raise our support. My youngest daughter, Jessica, had become very close to her. Jessica is very affectionate. She has golden brown hair, brown eyes, and an eagerness to hug and be hugged. Jessica's personality fit my mother totally, and I knew it was going to be exceptionally difficult for them to part.

I went to say good-bye to my grandmother. She is a shut-in and has crippling arthritis. She is unable to walk; her feet, legs, arms, and hands are curled up into a kind of misshapen "C". However, she is able to speak and her mind is good, but she is completely incapable of caring for herself. I wondered, would I see her again on earth, or was this the last time? I couldn't know.

I was convinced that these questions were coming from Satan in an attempt to defeat and prevent me from doing the work God had assigned me to do. Now I know that some would say fear and doubt are sinful. It is true the Word of God tells us not to fear. This is because fear has great potential to destroy us. However, fear can also strengthen us when we commit it to the Lord. We are human and we will have fear. It is by allowing the grace of God to conquer our fears that we learn to trust in Him and not ourselves. Perhaps this has something to do with what Paul meant when he spoke to the Romans in Romans 11:20, *"...Be not high-minded but fear."* It is a proud man who fears nothing, but it is a spiritual man who learns to trust God in spite of his fear.

Whatever your opinion, there was for certain a very real struggle going on inside of me. On one hand I knew what to do, but on the other hand I was faced with doubts on this last day. The dream of being a missionary had come to pass. Now I was beginning to face the reality of it. We had purchased one-way tickets with no money for a return fare. We were going to a place where we didn't really know anyone. I was taking my wife and children to a place I knew little about except for what I had read and the information I had obtained from other missionaries. What was I doing?

All too soon it was time to leave. My Pastor, with his cheerful personality, tried to ease the tension everyone felt by telling some of his corny jokes, but today they were of little help. We loaded the dark brown van with our carefully taped bags and packages. Once everything was packed, it was time to say our final good-bye. Tears flowed as we hugged each precious person and told them how much we loved them and how much we would miss them. They in turn said the same to us. Once in the van we were ready to start our journey. We were backing down the driveway when suddenly Jessica (my youngest daughter) shouted, "Stop!" She opened the van door, jumped out, and ran as fast as she could into the arms of her grandmother (whom she called MawMaw Betty) to get one more hug and to say "I love you" one more time. The scene almost broke my heart. As I took her little hand and led her back to the van I could not look back again.

This was only the beginning of tests we would face as missionaries. It is in situations such as this that the missionary and his family must be convinced of their calling. It is an absolute certainty that the missionary will be tested, thus the foreign missionary must be prepared. He must have determination that he will finish what he has begun. He must be strong enough to endure in most difficult and trying circumstances. Satan will bring doubts and discouragement. But, this is the time when the missionary will need to fall down on his knees and ask God to free his mind of these discouragements. It is only the grace and power of God that will give him the strength to continue to move ahead with his work for God. The missionary must remember that he is a soldier in the army of God; and as a soldier, he must endure hardships from time to time.

11 Timothy 2:1-4 reminds us we need to be strong in the grace of God which is our only hope for a continued and successful ministry for the Lord Jesus Christ. It states:

8

*"Thou therefore, my son, be strong in the grace that is in Christ Jesus. And the things that thou hast heard of me among many witnesses, the same commit thou to faithful men, who shall be able to teach others also. Thou therefore endure hardness, as a good soldier of Jesus Christ. No man that warreth, entangleth himself with the affairs of this life that he may please him who hath chosen him to be a soldier."*

This is the missionary's work and the verses above can give assurance and rest when enduring the difficulties of missionary life. Missionaries have given themselves to commit the gospel to those in need. Therefore, this mission supercedes earthly affairs. It requires strength and determination found only in grace. God has provided everything needed to do the work.

The questions that the aspiring missionary must ask are, "Am I willing?" "Is Christ truly preeminent?' Do I love Christ more than the comforts, care, and relationships of the world?" If the answer to these questions is "yes," then he is a candidate for missions. A person who cannot give an affirmative answer to these questions will have great difficulty serving as a missionary.

# CHAPTER TWO

## - Surprise!  Surprise! -

*"By faith Abraham, when he was called to go out*

*into a place which he should after receive for an*

*inheritance obeyed; and he went out,*

*not knowing whither he went."*

Hebrews 11:8

I will never forget the feeling of excitement when our plane touched down at Jomo Kenyatta Airport, Nairobi, Kenya. We had said our good-byes at Dulles Airport to our pastor and his family. Now only 20 hours later we were at our land of promise.

It was late when we arrived. We met a missionary who lived near the city. He drove us to a guest house where we would spend our first night in Kenya. During the ride I looked out the car windows and saw large skyscrapers. I remember thinking that this is like the USA. Indeed Nairobi is a modern, bustling city like many in America, but upon closer investigation I could see there were vast differences.

The following morning we were rushed up for breakfast by our missionary friend; then given a short tour of Nairobi on the way to our next destination, "the train station."

Upon our arrival at the train station we found we had arrived three hours early so we had to wait with our 14 pieces of luggage stacked up like a wall in the middle of the train station.

As we waited my eyes surveyed all the unusual sights. Standing only a few feet from us were three African ladies. They were dressed in what appeared to be large colorful scarves which they had wrapped and tied around themselves in a most peculiar way. One of them

11

had a small baby wrapped in another one of these scarves, which in some mysterious way was tied to her from the neck allowing the baby to hang suspended from her back in a very secure position. All of these ladies (even the one with the baby) were balancing their bags on their heads. As they moved and spoke there was not even a hint that the bags might fall off (they never did!).

In another part of the station there was a small boy with about 4 or 5 goats. "What is that boy going to do with those goats?", I asked the missionary with me.

"He is going to take them with him on the train."

"On the train!" I exclaimed. This clearly caused me a bit of concern as the train ride would take about 12 hours, and the possibility of sitting next to five goats for that length of time was not very appealing to my nose's delicate sense of smell. The missionary, seeing my concern, laughed and informed me that we would be in another part of the train. "Whew!" I was relieved.

Since we had such a long wait I decided to go in search of Cokes for the family. Street vendors were everywhere selling everything from souvenirs to live chickens. The vendor from which I bought the Cokes had a radio. I remember how surprised I was to hear a Dolly Parton and Kenny Rogers' song coming from it. I don't know why, but I guess I expected to hear something along the lines of "oba dooba oba dooba dooba dooba oba oba dooba." Imagine Kenny Rogers in Africa. Upon my return with the Cokes, I saw a strange and bewildered look on Tammy's face. The only way I can describe it is a look of "Where am I? Why am I here? and "What am I going to do to survive?" She didn't know it, but I felt the same way too. This place on the surface looked like any city in America, but it was not America. The people did not understand me and worse, I did not understand them (even when they spoke in English). Finally, the train pulled into the station, and we were allowed to board.

The train ride turned out to be a pleasant experience. We had our own compartment with large windows which allowed us to see the beautiful countryside of Kenya on our way to Mombasa where we would be stationed as missionaries. During the daylight hours we saw much of the wildlife for which the country is so famous. We were glued to the window pointing at the likes of giraffe, antelope, and zebra.

All through the night we rode. The train made several stops for loading and unloading. During one of these stops a small boy stood at the tracks below our window. He looked to be about five years old. He was dressed only in a pair of torn, dirty underpants. Obviously he was hungry. My heart reached out to help him but I could not leave the train. Suddenly I remembered a candy bar in my bag. We threw it out the window to him. I will always remember the look of joy on his face as he ran away holding tightly to this piece of gold he had been given. My thought was, as he departed, that though earthly suffering is terrible, it is even worse to suffer life on earth and then suffer for eternity without the precious gift of God's Son. I understood at that moment more than ever before the importance of the message we must carry to the starving souls of sinful men.

Soon the train was on its way again, and the gentle motion rocked us all to sleep. It was a good feeling to be in God's will.

We arrived the next morning at the town of Mombasa. The town lies on an island separated from the mainland by a channel which forms the harbor. Immediately I was struck by the intense heat and humidity, which caused profuse sweating without expending much effort. Contrary to my anticipation, this was a fairly large town. There were many old buildings lining the streets. Everywhere I looked I saw people. I remember wondering, "What are they all doing and where are they going?" Some thickly-muscled young men were pulling large wooden wagons filled with goods to different shops and markets within the town. In front of the shops on almost every street I noticed beggars: some men, some women, some children. Upon closer observation, I saw that many were victims of leprosy, and that parts of their bodies had already been destroyed by this hideous disease. All of them were asking for a handout and in some areas we had to step over them to continue. The town was very dirty, and near the market areas there were strong and sometimes nauseating odors. Some people had made these dirty streets their homes, and as I have witnessed, actually gained subsistence from the garbage heaps. Never before had I witnessed such a sight.

Although the town had these disadvantages, it also had a strange charm. The old historical buildings with their flat roofs, dingy white walls, and hand-carved wooden doors, the many Mosques and Hindu Temples with their beautiful architecture, the street vendors, the huge open air vegetable market, and the young men pulling those wooden wagons all combined to form a charmingly interesting and unexpected picture.

As we continued we were told we were not quite home yet. We were informed that we would need to cross the channel from Mombasa to the mainland to reach the small town called Likoni where we would be living. The only way this could be done was by ferry.

Likoni was only about two miles away from Mombasa, but because of the waiting for the ferry, it took us one hour and five minutes to get there. Finally, we reached Likoni. Likoni was totally different from Mombasa. The town was bathed in sunshine and lay on the edge of the channel with its still waters shimmering in the sunlight. There were no tall buildings or large shops. The shops and buildings were mostly built from wooden poles, mud, and coconut tree leaves (called makuti). Inside Likoni away from the shopping areas, there were nice homes made from block and plaster. Most of these were owned by wealthy blacks, whites, or Asians. One thing I found interesting was how the small grass or makuti houses were interspersed together with these large homes. So you would see a large plaster house with a neighbor who lived in a small hut. All of these houses were set amid waving palms, tall coconut trees, and sumptuous fruit trees.

One particular house situated in this setting was the home of an older missionary couple. It was their responsibility to help us adjust to this new life of ours. Their house was a beautiful little flat set right on the seashore. I will call them "Bob and Jane." Bob had graying brown hair and his back was slightly crooked as the result of some childhood illness. He had a serious and determined attitude toward his work. Jane's personality was more lively. She enjoyed engaging in light conversation and was friendly. Both of these good people quickly became our friends and helped us greatly in learning about this new land we were in.

Bob and Jane were the ones who took us to see the house we would be living in. It was a musty old place built high up on concrete pillars. It had large windows with no screens on them. (In Africa, windows usually do not have screens, something I don't quite understand; because to me, it surely must be the insect capital of the world.) The furniture was well worn and looked as if it came from a 1930's movie. Outside, there was a large yard with plenty of playing space for the children. It had

16

a beautiful garden with all kinds of flowering trees and shrubs. Also, there were trees full of different fruits such as papaya, passion, banana, and oranges. Near the house there were three large concrete tanks. It was explained that water was a problem in Likoni, and these tanks were built to catch rainwater during the rainy seasons. Therefore, we would need to learn to conserve water since this might be all we would have during the dry season.

Looking back at the house from the yard, I could see our car parked between the concrete pillars supporting the house. The car had been purchased for us by the missionaries with funds we had sent prior to our arrival. It was a 1979 bright orange Volkswagen Van, which we affectionately called "the pumpkin." It would be our companion on many adventures in the years to come. This was our new home.

Home was not everything we had imagined it to be, but we had to adjust to the differences between imagination and reality. This is important, because even the best investigation of the future field will be distorted by pictures and ideas in the mind. Therefore flexibility is important. Flexibility is the ability to accept a thing even though it is not as imagined to be. For many missionaries discouragement sets in at this very beginning point. Perhaps they imagined they would be in the bush, but this is a town. Perhaps they are in the bush, but they did not realize what being in the bush would mean. Perhaps they expected and wanted to live in a hut, but not so. Perhaps they wanted a nice house but were given a hut. Perhaps, they thought they would have a car, but none could be found. Surprises and disappointments occur upon arrival. The willingness to adapt will determine your staying power. Staying power and perspective are needed.

Staying power together with the ability to keep everything in perspective are of the utmost importance. God has called the missionary to a work; many times our dreams and expectations about the place of ministry have little to do with that work. For example, what does the color or softness of a chair have to do with helping people to hear the message of Christ? Things must be kept in perspective. It will be a great help to remember God is in control of these differences, minor or major, and He is continuing to work them for good (Rom. 8:28). If things are different than imagined, there is surely a reason why. The missionaries' responsibility, then, is to adapt and accept these differences.

# CHAPTER THREE

## - Get Ready!  Get Set! ... Wait!

*"But let patience have her perfect work, that ye*

*may be perfect and entire, wanting nothing."*
James 1:4

Once all of our bags were unpacked and our things put in place, we were ready to get involved in the ministry. Only three days after our arrival in Mombasa, the regional missionary meeting was held within our organization. It was at this meeting that we were told our participation in the ministry would be limited. We wouldn't be allowed to work in any of the national churches or at the Mission Bible School. We were told during our first year our primary concern should be to study the Kiswahili language and to learn the culture of the people.

Now, I knew that our major concentration during our first year on the field would be learning the language, but somehow I thought in addition I would be given some real opportunities for service. These opportunities I'd hoped for were not to be.

As one might imagine, this was a real blow to me. I had spent almost four years raising funds to reach this place, and now I was being told I couldn't do anything. I did not understand. Did these other missionaries dislike me? Did they believe that I was inferior? Would I ever be accepted by them? Why were they limiting me? I just couldn't understand.

Although I didn't understand why I had been limited, my wife and I continued our language studies. Each day we became more familiar with the Kiswahili language. We understood that knowledge of this language would be essential to an effective ministry; for even though there were educated people who knew English, most of the older people, children, and those in rural areas did not.

So we studied. We studied by class work every afternoon. We studied by labeling all of the furniture, doors, windows, and walls with their Kiswahili names. We studied by visiting the market and attempting to buy vegetables in the language. We studied by conversing with national people whom we had met and by listening to tapes. We memorized nearly 500 vocabulary words. Sometimes I would go to sleep at night and see vocabulary words in my dreams.

These dreams of vocabulary words were also accompanied by dreams of working with nationals to spread the gospel and primarily for me to begin establishing a local church. This desire to become more involved kept barking at my mind like an angry watchdog. Why couldn't I have a chance to work? There was a Bible School educating nationals. The classes were in English and they needed help. So, why not let me assist? I could do this and language too, but the opportunity was not to come. Resentment began to build in me toward these other missionaries.

My resentment took two courses. First, I began to find things wrong in the other missionaries' work. Second, I found an ally in another missionary. I will call him "Mark." He had major disagreements with the other missionaries. Mark began to tell me horror stories of how he had been treated. He told me of how these "co-laborers" had mistreated and misused funds, etc. As I listened, I began to use these things to build my list of complaints. In the regular mission meetings, I heard people speak angrily about Mark. I couldn't believe the things I was hearing. Mark was a young, clean-cut graduate of a major Christian university. He worked diligently at trying to establish a church. He seemed very dedicated and all alone. Yet, the others criticized him at almost every turn. This was missions? These were the spiritual giants I had seen as a youth in church? I grew more and more resentful.

In the ninth month of my first year on the field, my resentment had almost reached a peak. I was talking to my wife about giving up and going back to the USA. It was during this ninth month that the Lord revealed some things to me.

First, I began to see some inconsistencies in Mark and the things he had told me. I came to discover that Mark had some definite problems that were not the result of the other missionaries. Many of the things he had told me simply were not true. Additionally, some of the things he was now saying bordered on the ridiculous. Up to this time, Mark had continually complained that the missionaries would not allow him to defend himself and face them with his accusations against them. In one of the regular mission meetings, I stated that Mark would like to face them all with his accusations and defend himself. All agreed that he could do this. It was decided that I should tell him the day to come and face them. Up this point, Mark had stated that he just wanted one opportunity to expose them. But now, with the opportunity he refused!. This was the beginning of my breakdown of confidence in what he had told me. Later, I discovered that most of his stories were untrue.

The realization that Mark was in fact a "trouble-maker" who should not have been on the field led me to my second realization. This realization was that Mark was the last missionary to come before me. These other missionaries had become frightened. They did not know if I was another "Mark." Perhaps I would bring more problems; they couldn't know for sure. Also, the field's work with the nationals was experiencing problems. These problems were centering around one particular missionary and one national pastor. The missionaries were protecting me from potential discouragement because of this problem and how it could influence me further. As I began to see their reasons for leaving me without involvement, my list of problems began to seem trivial. I realized that my resentment and bitterness came from a lack of understanding.

Understanding one's lack of understanding is essential for the first-year missionary. He is in a new surrounding. Perhaps he doesn't know the background of those on his team. When and if restrictions are put on him, he should be careful to discover and understand the real reasons. Listening to one's emotions and reasoning by limited knowledge can only lead to misunderstanding and sin.

The heart can be kept from sin in this first year by understanding seven basic truths concerning the first year on the field:

1- Language is of utmost importance. If you are to ever be able to communicate the gospel effectively and build relationships with nationals, you must know their language.

2- Culture must be understood. Works have been destroyed because a missionary did not understand the culture of the people and adapt to it. It takes a minimum of one year even to begin to be familiar with a culture.

3- Understand missionaries are human. They can make mistakes. Be Forgiving!

4- Guard your heart. Protect it by confessing bitterness.

5- Do what you can with approval of your mission. Any work done for Christ is important.

6- Be open. When you don't know why, ASK!

7- Trust. Your time will come, so hang in
   there.


   Every new missionary has a God-given sense of urgency, but this urgency must be tempered by allowing oneself time to understand. In years ahead, the missionary will appreciate this time spent learning and adapting.

# CHAPTER FOUR

## - Detour -

*"For who hath known the mind of the Lord?*

*or who hath been His counselor?"*
Romans 11:34

It was very good that I began to have understanding concerning my problems on the field in the ninth month. If not, what happened in the tenth month might have completely defeated me.

On Friday afternoon at about six o'clock P.M., our telephone rang. I picked up the receiver and said, "Hello." The voice at the other end was my brother. Immediately, in a cracking voice he said, "Don't worry." This alone was enough to tell me something was wrong. He continued to tell me that my mother had gone to the doctor that week. She had been given a test and now that test had come back. It was positive. She had cancer. Cancer! A small word, but oh the fear it brings into the mind. I asked, "Is it bad?" His answer was they did not know yet, but it seemed to be serious. After hearing this (although I'm not sure why), I began to deny that it could be serious. I just couldn't believe that my mother could have cancer, and if it truly was cancer it couldn't be very serious. After all, she was only 56 years old. After some further discussion, my brother said he would call again as soon as they received more details on her condition.

After hanging up the receiver, I told my wife the news. She responded with shock and asked, "What are we going to do?" I told her there was nothing we could do except wait for more information, but that I was sure it was some kind of mistake. "Let's not worry until we know for sure what is wrong," I said.

Three weeks passed before my brother called again, which was fine because I figured no news was good news. When I answered the phone and heard the voice of my brother, I was convinced that the news would be good; but the news was not good. He informed me that mom's cancer was widespread with little hope of her survival. I asked if I should come home. He said that mom did not want me to come home yet because she didn't want me to leave the Lord's work unless absolutely necessary. These words spoke to my heart about the faith of my mother. Many times on the field we experience trials and wonder why we have to take this stand and do what God has called us to do under difficult circumstances, as if no one at home faces problems or trials. But here was my mother who was facing a battle with cancer, but also kept a real concern that the work of God not stop. I agreed that I would wait until mom asked for me to come home.

As I finished talking to my brother, I asked God to please give everyone at home special grace to cope with this situation. I also asked the Lord to help me to have the strength and courage to do the right thing when called for.

The right thing, I thought, what is the right thing? If needed, should I go home or should I stay on the field? What does God want me to do? I knew that it wouldn't be long before I would have to answer these questions.

I discovered my answer to these questions less than one month later when my brother phoned again, "Mom is dying". The doctor says she probably has 3-6 months to live. She wants you to come home." Instantly, I knew what I had to do. I began making arrangements to leave for America as soon as possible. Within two weeks I would be home. But what would I face when I got there?

The flight back to the States was long and tiring. Upon reaching where my mom was staying, I faced my first trial. My wife went in to see my mother first. After a while, I was called to come in. What I saw was shocking. She was very pale and thin. Her full dark hair had almost all fallen out. I tried to cover my shock and speak as if everything was okay.

I truly believed that everything was going to be okay. I was home to take care of her, and I knew that the Lord was able to heal her. So, I determined that she would get better.

With this belief, I encouraged Mom to continue treatments. When she returned for her treatments, my brother and I met with her doctor. He informed us that treatments had a slight chance to help her, but that chance was less than 25% since she was already in stage four cancer.

"A slight chance!" These were the words I'd hoped to hear. I was even more convinced that God would make her better. But she did not get better. We were in and out of the hospital for the next four months. Yes, I still believed there would be a turn around. During one of Mom's stays at the hospital, my brother Rick and I decided she should go to a major university hospital nearby which had a cancer research facility. Mom reluctantly agreed to go as a last attempt to get help.

For a while, Mom seemed to get better and I was very encouraged. She even began to talk about what she was going to do when she got better. One particular day I was very surprised when she told me she was hungry and wanted a pizza. (Up to this time, she had lost her appetite completely.) I was overjoyed. Tammy and I took her downstairs, to the cafeteria. In the cafeteria there was a pizza parlor. I cannot describe how I felt at this time. All that I was seeing gave me great encouragement. I was on top of a mountain emotionally.

Unfortunately, this mountain-top experience was not to last. The next day Mom was scheduled for a minor operation to install a device into a heart artery which would enable her to take her medication more easily. During the operation, something went wrong. Mom's blood pressure dropped to almost zero and she was not expected to survive. After waiting for almost ten hours of not knowing what was wrong, a nurse came into the waiting room. She told us of Mom's complications and that if we wanted to see her again we'd better go to ICU. recovery immediately. At ICU recovery, Ricky, our wives, and I were allowed to go in. There was a team of doctors working on Mom. One of the doctors told us she probably wouldn't survive another hour. Ricky and I both had tear-filled eyes. I wondered, "how can this be? Yesterday we were eating pizza together!"

At about that time, Mom awoke. She took my hand and told me not to worry. She said she has seen an angel and he said it would be all right. She told me to continue serving the Lord because nothing else really counts in this world. Then she spoke to Ricky. We were not there more than four or five minutes before we were told we had to leave so the medical team could do their job. All we could do was wait.

What a long wait it was! All through the night up until 5:30 p.m. the next day. Finally, a nurse came in and told us Mom was being moved from recovery to regular ICU. She was still critical but well enough that she could · be moved. As I went in to see Mom, I saw many tubes and cords connected to her body. I called her name, but the nurse informed me that she was in a coma. So I told her I loved her, then I prayed for her and left to tell the others outside of her condition.

There was a small hotel next to the hospital where Tammy and I secured a room to stay in until Mom was out of danger or "?." We stayed there for one week; then all of a sudden Mom was awake and could be moved to a regular room in the hospital. What a relief! We stayed in the hospital room with Mom all day, and Tammy stayed the night there with her. I went back to Mom's house to sleep, physically tired and emotionally spent.

It was that night when I experienced an unexpected trial of my faith. It was about 9:30 p.m. when the telephone rang. I picked up the receiver and one of my "supporting" pastors was on the other end. He asked how my Mom was and quickly got to the business at hand. He informed me that I was out of the will of God by coming home to take care of my mother. He told me that God expected me to be on the field; and then he quoted Matthew 8:22, *"follow me and let the dead bury their dead."* He further explained that my responsibility was to the work in Kenya not to my mother. He was sorry she was sick, but they would no longer support me. My first reaction was anger, but thank the Lord, I was just too tired to give much response. I told him to do what seemed right to him and the Lord would take care of me. I hung up the phone and went to sleep completely over-whelmed by that phone call.

Within the next couple of months, I would get more of the same by at least two more pastors and one missionary. But, by far, most of the supporting pastors, churches, and my fellow missionaries were in support of my decision, for which I am grateful. I could have never endured emotionally without the Lord's encouragement through the support of those pastors and churches.

Concerning Mom's condition, although she recovered from the operation, her cancer continued to worsen. By this time her weight was at around 85 pounds. One day the doctor came in and told us there was nothing more he could do to help Mom. He was sure that death was inevitable within the next week or month. This was devastating news, but I was amazed that Mom took it as if she already had accepted that fact. (Which in truth she probably had.) Mom told me she wanted to go home. She had had nothing but problems in that hospital; now she wanted some peace.

The doctor contacted the area hospice agency, which were a great help in preparing us to take care of Mom. My brother Ricky had gotten a hospital bed for Mom. Everything was ready when we brought her home. She would not have to see a hospital again.

Tammy and I stayed with Mom in the house. Tammy assumed the part of nurse and gave Mom her daily injections as well as attempting to feed her through a tube in her stomach. Three more months passed and Mom lost weight down to 45 pounds. By this time Mom could not walk and her memory was fading. Sometimes she was coherent and at other times not. Often I would go into her room to talk and pray with her. My daughter

Jessica would climb up on the bed and talk with her, which always seemed to give Mom great pleasure.

All during this time, my brother's wife was pregnant. Mom stated that she hoped to live long enough to see the baby. She did and we have pictures of her holding her one and only grandson, named Coley.

Sometimes Mom would get restless and I would carry her to the living room where we could sit and listen to Christian music. She enjoyed very much coming into the living room with the whole family. Unfortunately, she would tire and have to be carried back to her bed for rest and quiet after only a few minutes.

One night after a particularly restless day where Mom would want to be carried to the living room, back to the bedroom, and then back to the living room and so forth, she became more serious. Her breathing became very shallow and we noticed her eyes were looking a bit strange.

Immediately we called the hospice nurse. She came out and examined Mom and told us she was dying. I quickly called my brother and my Mom's sisters so they could come and say good-bye. By the time they arrived, I believe Mom was already entering another realm. She was talking but not to us. She would reach out her hands; but when we tried to hold them, she would push us away and say, "Not you, him!"

This was the longest night of my entire life. At one point I thought, "Maybe they are wrong; perhaps she's not dying." But as the night progressed, I realized she was going to die, and I began to feel anxious about it. I don't know whether it was God's gracious way of preparing me or not, but I knew she had experienced enough pain. Now it was time for relief. I knew that in the arms of her wonderful Savior she would find that relief. Comfort, rest, and strength would all return the instant she felt his embrace. Could it have been He whom she was reaching for in that room? I don't know, but we all felt a presence in her room that could not be explained. The hospice nurses said it was the presence of love. I don't know exactly what they meant, but I agree. I do believe love was there. The love of family, but also a greater love. It was the presence of Him who is love. The Lord of Lords and King of Kings -- Mom's blessed Savior. I believe she was reaching towards Him.

We all stood by the bed and one by one told Mom good-bye. I told Mom I would see her when I get home so keep a lookout. Then, I took her arm and began to rub it as I sang to her like she used to sing to me when I was a sick child. I felt the coldness come into her arm and it was over. Mom had gone home. We all gathered around her bed, held hands, and sang, "*Amazing grace, how sweet the sound that saved a wretch like me. I once was lost but now I'm found, was blind but now I see.*" Then we sang the last verse to remind us where Mom had gone.

35

*"When we've been there ten thousand years, bright shining as the sun. We've no less days to sing God's praise than when we first begun."* I will always be grateful that I was with her at that last moment. I had made the right decision.

Yes, for me that was the right decision. I'm not saying it would have been correct for everyone. Some might have taken a different route which would been God's way for them to go. But, this was God's detour for me. Even though this was a detour in my path as a missionary, it was a benefit to me. Imagine driving on a dark night on a road where a bridge is out. If there was no detour sign, it could mean disaster. In the same way, God sends detours from time to time. Perhaps one's path has been carefully mapped out. But God knows he needs to take a different way, so He sends him a detour.

Therefore, one's responsibility is to determine the way God wants him to go now. Everyone will not go the same way, but everyone must make a decision when the detour sign is in front of him.

Also, one must be ready to live with his choice. Is he aware of the consequences of his actions? Is he sure this is the way God wants him to go? What about criticism and conflict. These are questions one must consider in his choice of a detour, because he will have to live with his decision the rest of his life.

# CHAPTER FIVE

## - Back on Track -

*"A man's heart deviseth his way:*

*but the Lord directeth his steps. "*

Proverbs 16:9

Within a short time after my mother's homegoing, we returned to Kenya. Upon reaching Likoni, it felt as if we had never really left. We began to put the events of the last year behind and to press on with what God had for us now.

What God had for us immediately was to clean the house. It had been vacant for the whole year and was filthy. In every corner there were cobwebs. The roof had developed a leak which caused the growth of mold and mildew on the walls. We had hired a teenage boy to come and clean while we were away, but it seemed as though he had not been very faithful.

After getting the house back into shape, we discovered the same old problems with the area had gotten worse. One problem centered around water. The government was no longer providing water to Likoni directly. Therefore, it meant I would spend all day at least two days per week driving back and forth from a water collection point, filling two 55-gallon drums in order to keep us in water. In addition to this, our roof was leaking during the rainy season, which gave us more water than we wanted (in our living room). Then, the sewers backed up because of insufficient water to flush out the lines. All of this, and the fact that our landlord did not seem interested in correcting the problems, caused us to decide it was time for a move.

We began our search for a new house with prayer. We wanted the Lord to lead us to the place of His choosing to begin a ministry for Him. After asking God's guidance, our physical search began. We visited real estate agents, checked ads in the newspaper, and followed up on leads given us by friends.

We viewed many houses -- some we liked, some we didn't. It seemed that either the monthly payment was too high or there was poor security, which was a main consideration, because burglaries are very common in poorly protected homes. We searched from place to place for almost a month.

Finally, our search seemed to come to an end when we found a small bungalow in the town of Nyali. Nyali is a small upper class area just outside of Mombasa. We viewed the house and it seemed to be just right. We met with the realtor, signed an agreement, and made a deposit. We were about to move in when the realtor called to inform us that the owner had decided not to rent the house. They returned our deposit and we were devastated. We had given our notice to leave our current house, and new renters were coming at the end of the week.

As the end of the week approached, we began to look furiously for a house. During the course of the week, a realtor said he wanted to take us to see a house for rent in Mtwapa, a small rural town north of Mombasa.

As we drove towards Mtwapa, the scenery changed. No longer could we see the big buildings and the crowds of the city. In Mtwapa, I saw a town reminiscent of what the old west towns might have looked like (minus the grass roofs). When we saw the house, it was beautiful. It was a ranch-style house made of block and plaster. It had a round tower built on the side made of coral stones. It had three bedrooms, which was perfect for my family. But it was so far from town. What if someone got sick? It could take us 45 minutes to an hour to get to the hospital. Shopping would also be a problem. Also, it had a huge open field beside it which I saw as a security problem because there was no fence around the compound. Last, the price was high. The monthly rent was about two and a half times the rent we were paying in Likoni. Therefore, we decided this was not the place for us. We continued searching.

Our searching took us to see another real estate agent. This agent took us to see several places; then he said he had one special place he wanted us to see. He took us to that same house in Mtwapa. We explained we had seen it already and weren't interest. Yet none of the other houses became available to us for one reason or another. The week was coming to a close.

It was two days before we had to be out of the house. In desperation, we went to see one more real estate agent who was recommended to us. This agent said he had a special place to show us. We got in his car and he promptly proceeded to Mtwapa. That's right! The same house again! We explained to this man that we had already seen this house twice, and although we thought it was beautiful, it was unacceptable for us. He asked our reasons why. I explained that the main reason was it had no fenced compound which left it open for burglary. He stated he would call the owner to ask if he would agree to build a fence. I said that if he agreed, we would take the house. The owner agreed and we moved into the house.

From the beginning, we fell in love with our new home and the little town of Mtwapa. It turned out that the town had many of the things we needed. It was also a friendly and comparatively safe town. As I think back, I'm grateful that God reserved this place for us.

Almost immediately we began meeting people. We met a mother and her daughter. We informed them we wanted to begin having a Bible study in our house. They agreed to come. The following Sunday was to be our first meeting. I put a sign on our gate inviting people to our fellowship and listed the time.

At our first meeting, there were my wife, my three children, the woman and her daughter, and me. We continued these meetings with just the seven of us for two months. Then, a young man joined the study with us.

After about two weeks, he received Christ as his Savior. Another month passed and an older man joined us. His name was Simon. After three weeks of attending the services, he was saved. I did not know it at the time, but God had a purpose in bringing in Simon. He was an expert mason and carpenter; and within a year and a half, his talents would be used in building our church.

Now, there were nine of us. We went on for another three months with just our small band. I began to get discouraged. Then one particular Sunday, two men came to the house and asked about the Bible study. The one man informed me he had just moved into the area and was looking for a place to worship. He stated that his family would come on the following Sunday to worship with us. I thought to myself, "Praise the Lord! This will probably be about four or five more people." To my surprise, when Sunday came, I saw a family of about 15 people coming to the church.

One by one on different Sundays, I saw each member in that family trust Christ as Savior and Lord. From this point our meetings took off. A woman named Susan joined our fellowship. She was saved and after church would go home and tell her Muslim husband what had been taught. He became curious about all she was telling him and began coming to listen for himself. Within a few months, he too received Christ. Our church was growing.

At about this time we had approximately 30-40 people meeting in the living room of our house. We decided to try to rent a place to meet in the main part of Mtwapa town. We found a small hut made of plywood and tin. We rented it for about $25.00 per month and began meeting there. I was very thankful to God for overruling my will and bringing us to this place.

In missions, as well as any other work, we as believers must be open to God's leadership and direction. One must have an open heart and seeing eyes to the will of God. We have the capacity to devise our own way, but the wise will make God's leading their direction.

I believe that many times we go in the direction we think is best and God, in His sovereignty, permits this even though He knows a better direction if we would only follow His gentle leading. The fact that you do not go the best way does not mean you are out of God's will, but it does mean that there could have been a better way for you if you had been open to His direction.

Is this a biblical concept? That one could be led to the better option of God's will if he would be open to it. It is, if we remember the fact that God is not only the God of what is, but of what could have been if certain conditions were met. Remember what Jesus said in Matthew 11:21, *"Woe unto thee, Chorazin! woe unto thee Bethsaida! for if the mighty works which were done in you, had been done in Tyre and Sidon, they would have repented long ago in sackcloth and ashes."*

43

Therefore, it is clear that one must be ever vigilant to obey the leading of God as you make decisions in life and ministry. We must seek His best for us.

# CHAPTER SIX

## - The Blessing of Opposition -

*"But it came to pass, that when Sanballat heard*

*that we builded the wall, he was wroth and took*

*great indignation, and mocked the Jews."*
Nehemiah 4:1

I was very happy to get this small hut in town. We decided that next Sunday we would move our services there. Tammy and I worked all week cleaning and preparing the place for services. We finally got it all cleaned up and it was ready. We brought our signboard and put it in front of the little church building. I got my first taste of opposition after putting up the sign. Many of the young men in the town were members of a non-Christian religion. Some of these were apathetic toward Christianity, but some were openly hostile.

Once the signboard was in place, some of these young men laughed. They mocked the little building and found it very amusing that this Christian missionary could only afford a little plywood hut for a meeting place. They, in turn, had large beautiful buildings complete with PA systems with which to preach their gospel.

They laughed and had a very good time with us. They often harassed our church people when they came to church. Although annoying, this was okay with us. At least we were making progress. In spite of the jeering of these "trouble-makers," our attendance continued to grow. Within one month our little hut was full. One of the people who was saved during this time was a man named Daniel.

I will never forget the first time I saw Daniel. He was a Rastafarian. For those who are unfamiliar with the term Rastafarian, let me try to give you a brief description of this lifestyle, as I understand it. The Rastafarian is captured in the midst of a hazy drug culture. He worships the former king Hailee Salasee of Ethiopia as the reincarnation of Christ. In an attempt to identify with the poor, they do not bathe regularly. They dress in old tattered clothing and do not cut or comb their hair. The dirty, matted, and uncombed hair is called "dreadlocks." The term "dreadlocks" refers to the fact that this present time and the hereafter is only something to dread. Misery and more misery is to come. Their life is one of spiritual deception, fatalism, witchcraft, and superstition. The late Caribbean singer Bob Marley is looked upon as a prophet for most of them. I don't know how deeply into this culture Daniel had gone, but you can imagine my surprise as on this particular Sunday, this somewhat untidy personage walked into the church. He came in very quietly, hands folded under his chin like a child praying by the bedside. He sat down and listened attentively. At the end of the service I asked, "If anyone would like to receive Jesus, please stand." Daniel stood and as we prayed, he had a personal encounter with the real Jesus Christ. God the Father had reached down into this crazy and mixed up "rasta" culture to reveal Himself to Daniel. His heart was captured by amazing grace, making him the member of a new group, a group called "Christians."

Daniel, realizing that in Jesus Christ he had no reason to dread the future, decided it was time to clean up and cut his hair. One morning Daniel came to my house. He explained he wanted to cut his hair and that his family was having a special ceremony for his dead father who had died one year earlier. At this ceremony, as the oldest son, he could give sacrifices to his father and be allowed to cut his hair.

He explained that these sacrifices involved cutting the throats of a goat, chicken, and cow over the grave of his father and allowing the blood to flow down to the body of his father. After that, he could tell his father while standing on top of the grave, "I have given you a goat, I have given you a chicken, and I have given you a cow, so don't bother me." Then he could sit in a chair on top of the grave and allow someone to cut his hair as it would not upset his dead father because of the sacrifices given.

Daniel was clearly concerned as a new Christian about doing this thing. He asked me what he should do? Now the answer to some might seem obvious, but let me give you a bit more insight. This ceremony was his people's tradition. This was Daniel's family. His mother, uncles, brothers, sister, etc. It was their tradition, handed down over the years. If he failed to comply with this custom, he could be ostracized from the family. This was the only way they would allow him freedom to change his appearance. To be forsaken by one's family is a serious problem. It means one could get no help in times of need. It means one's wife and children will not be cared for if anything happens to him. It means one loses all land that belongs to him because he has forsaken the ways of his family. I did not know what to tell him. So, I told him to help me pray about it and come again to see me the next day, and I would try to give an answer.

What answer could I give? I prayed that night for guidance and wisdom. How could Daniel please the Lord and his family? Then the Lord impressed me with an idea.

When Daniel came the next day, I shared with him my idea. I told him to go ahead with the ceremony, but tell everyone there that he was now a Christian. Tell them he knew that his dead father could not cause him problems and that his only trust was now in Christ. Therefore, out of respect and love for his father and his traditions and also for God, he would keep the ceremony, but only with these conditions. One, the animals would not be killed over the grave. They would not be used as a sacrifice. They would cook and eat them as a memorial feast. Two, Daniel would not address his father's spirit, but would say some words to all of the family in honor of his father. Three, he would cut his hair, but not on the grave. He went and he did these things, and it was well received by his family. Praise the Lord for His ever-present help in time of need!

Seeing God at work in the lives of people in this little "storefront" church did not endear us to our opposition. Clearly we were causing them much agitation. This resulted in a more physical kind of opposition.

This physical opposition took on various forms. One thing we could expect every Sunday was for some of these young men to pick up large sticks and beat them on the outside walls of our building during the service. Sometimes they would put their heads in the windows and shout mockingly, "Amen!, Praise the Lord, or Hallelujah!" Sometimes they would bring out radios and sit around the church with them in an attempt to drown out the message. One Sunday morning, we discovered a particularly disgusting sight. We got to the church early in order to dust and clean before the people came. Approaching the step in front of the door, we saw that it was covered with human dung. Obviously, it had been deposited there in the night as an insult and message to the church. Clearly not everyone wanted us there. We cleaned the disgusting mess and went on with the morning services.

The harassment continued, and occasionally while I was preaching, a large stick might fly in from the open door in front of the pulpit. Sunday morning harassment became a regular part of our worship experience.

After two and a half months at the hut, one particular Sunday everything came to a climax. I was just beginning to preach when one man in the church was called outside. He returned in a few minutes and informed I was needed outside. I turned the service over to someone else while I went out to see what was going on.

I was shocked when I saw that one of the women of the church had been grabbed by two big men and ordered to tell me to vacate that building at once.

The man who told her to tell us to leave was the owner of the land which the building sat on. We had rented from a man who owned the building but obviously he did not own the land. Apparently, it is not uncommon here for one person to own a building and another person to own the land it sits on.

The owner of the land was a member of the group causing us problems. He had been out of town and now he wanted "this church" off his property. He further went on to inform me that he would rather see a bar in that place than a church. He left us with no choice but to leave.

As I went back into the church, I felt very defeated. All of the strength had gone out of me, and I suddenly felt flushed and tired. I told the people this would be our last Sunday in the hut. We would begin meeting again at my house next week.

When the following Sunday arrived, I must admit I was still discouraged. The main reason was that I felt this was a step backward for the work. We had progressed out of my living room and into our own little building, only to be chased away. However, this discouragement did not last long because in that service we had more people come than in any service previously. Some said it was because they had heard about our problem and wanted us to know that not everyone in town was against the church. I knew that this was God's way of teaching me to trust Him. He had turned defeat into a victory and shown me again that He was running this program.

Yet, this was not the last time I would be discouraged. Discouragement comes from different places. Sometimes it comes from outside, as in the case of this non-Christian religious group. Yet, this is not where my next trial would come. It would come from my fellow missionaries.

Most missionaries would not hesitate to speak in favor of the indigenous church concept. Most believe that this is a biblical principle, but what does one mean when he speaks of indigenization?

To me, indigenization means establishing a self-governing and self-supporting work completely free of outside influence and aid. In the case of a church, it would mean that the national people govern and support their own ministry.

When speaking with my fellow missionaries about this concept, I found that some were supportive, but others flatly told me this was impossible to accomplish in this third world. I was informed that people of the third world had learned to be dependent, that they were too poor or too disorganized to support their own work. I was advised that no church or work would stand without outside support. Therefore, "indigenous" to these missionaries meant allowing nationals to govern their work, but never giving them the financial responsibilities.

The problem with this concept is this. What if the mission and missionaries need to pull out from the country? What will happen to these churches and ministries where the nationals have not learned or accepted the financial responsibility? The answer is simple. They are headed for trouble. None of these missionaries would deny the indigenous principle of missions, but there is a difference as to the meaning of the term. To some, indigenous could be self-governing but not necessarily self-supporting. I firmly believe that a work should be "fully indigenous." This means that it should be self-governing and self-supporting. I do not mean that the new church or ministry would not need help from donor funds in America or elsewhere; but I do believe that the funds should be used only in establishing a work at the beginning. Afterward the missionary should gradually withdraw these funds, placing and increasing the burden on the nationals to fill the gap.

In spite of being told that the particular tribe I was working with were poorer and less educated than some of the other tribes in Kenya and that establishing a strong, self-supporting church among them would be next to impossible, I determined with God's help this would be my method.

Determination is essential in work for God. One must know that he is in the will of God. This assurance of being in God's will with the work he is doing will help him to stand firm in opposition. Be assured opposition will come. Satan is ever vigilant to destroy what God is doing. Therefore, one must have a clear idea and conviction of the way God wants him to go.

With clear conviction, one's determination to accomplish his task will be strengthened. But without it, questions will arise as to what he is doing.

Questions will always arise in one's mind as to the path he should go on in any given task, but questions that bring one to defeat can be overcome by an understanding of what one wants to accomplish and the determination to see it through. One must know what he believes. Be sure of what he is to do. He must be willing to make adjustment to his ideas as needed, but never to compromise on the way he believes he is to go. He must be flexible on details but firm on his outcome.

What is meant by flexibility on details and firm on outcome? Sometimes in attempting to accomplish his God-given task, the missionary will implement procedures or practices he believes will help. Some of these will be beneficial and useful. Others, although good ideas to the missionary, are actually useless in furthering the work. They may be useless because of contrast in culture or abilities of the nationals to perform these given tasks. Therefore, the missionary will need to be flexible and seek a different method with which to accomplish his goal in a way which is more suitable to the people themselves. Therefore, the missionary has changed a detail, but his overall goal for the work has not changed. Thus, he has been flexible and firm in his determination. This ability is what separates those who quit early from those who see a project through to the finish.

Never forget, *"We can do all things through Christ who strengthens us."*

# CHAPTER SEVEN

## - A Place of Our Own -

*"Who is there among you of all his people? His*
*God be with him, and let him go up to Jerusalem,*
*which is in Judah, and build the house of*
*the Lord God of Israel, (He is the God,) which is*
*in Jerusalem. And whosoever remaineth in any*
*place where he sojourneth, let the men of his*
*place help him with silver, and with gold, and*
*with goods, and with beast, beside the freewill*
*offering for the house of God that is in Jerusalem."*
Ezra 1:3-4

With determination to do what I believed God called me to do, I began a series of fund-raising attempts. Every two or three weeks in our church meetings, we took up a special offering. I informed the people this offering would be used to buy land once we raised enough and found the right place.

I began the search for land after we had raised approximately 10,000/= shillings. I asked one of the more responsible men in the church to help me. He began searching while I kept a lookout also.

Getting land here is both easy and difficult. It is easy if the land is truly owned by the person who is presenting himself as the seller, but if he is not, look out! You could be headed for trouble.

I almost went head-on into trouble on one land prospect which I learned about from a national pastor in a nearby church. I thank the Lord for his intervention before I proceeded.

The problem is that there are many people who live on land which officially does not belong to them. Sometimes these people will see an opportunity to make money from some unsuspecting dupe.

In this case, I was the dupe they attempted to make money from. I was taken to see a beautiful wooded plot, on level ground, in the middle of a nice little community.

It was the perfect place for us to put a church building. The people told me I could purchase this land for only 10,000/= shillings (about 200.00 dollars), which was cheap, of course.

I was ready to grab at such a deal! I immediately put a deposit on this plot of 500/=shillings (about $10.00). Excitedly I went home to tell my wife about this wonderful plot. That night one of my missionary friends phoned. As we discussed different aspects of our ministries, I mentioned that I had found land. I told him of the great deal I had discovered, and as he listened, I could sense that he was uneasy about this deal.

He explained to me about the problem of conmen who will sell land that really isn't theirs. He explained in detail the procedure of how I could go about discovering whether this deal was on the up and up or not.

I followed his directions and soon discovered that the deal was crooked. Those men did not actually own the land, but were squatters. I lost 500/= shillings, but that's not as bad as losing it all. I thank God for this other missionary's help in that matter.

Not long after that, the man in the church I had told to look for land presented me with a real bona fide sell of land. We made arrangements to see the plot with the owner's representative.

The plot was 50' x'100'. It stood in the center of a large open field. The price was 90,000/= shillings (about 1800.00 dollars). This price was very high, I thought, but still it was the real thing.

I told the representative I would need time to think about it. He agreed to wait one week for my decision. I told the people of our church about the plot. We all wanted it. They had an immediate fundraising and raised another 10,000/= shillings. Now we had 20,000/= shillings, but we still needed 70,000/= shillings more. Through prayer, I decided that God would have me make a call to my home church in America. I called and told my pastor of how we had been chased from our hut and had returned to my house for meetings. I told him how we had found a plot and that we needed approximately $1,500.00 to purchase it.

My pastor said that they were in revival that week. Therefore, when he arrived at church that night he would present this need to the church.

The next day I received a call from my pastor informing me that the church had voted unanimously to give the money directly to our little church for the land. I thanked him and hung up the phone feeling jubilant.

The following day, I called and told the plot owner's representative that I was coming to give a 20,000/= shilling deposit and would pay the balance within two weeks. This would allow time to receive the funds from our home church in the States.

Within two weeks we had paid for the plot in full, and within one month we had the official title deed to the land. It was time to start building.

We began by buying materials. Mr. Simon, the man who was a mason, put up a small tin shack and lived on the plot to protect, from thieves, the items which we bought. We bought a truck load of blocks with money we raised after one month. Another month we bought cement, with more money which had been raised. It all stayed on the plot until we could afford to buy water for mixing. Once the water money was raised, we laid the foundation. This finished every item we had bought. Materials were expensive and even though everyone was giving, we could never complete the project on our own.

But we were not on our own. The Lord was with us. He had caused some of our supporting churches in the USA to hear about our building program. Funds began to come in every month which were a great help in purchasing materials.

During the time that we were trying to get enough materials together to lay the concrete slab, my pastor and his family came to Kenya to visit with us and see the work.

He arrived just in time for the laying of the slab. The men of the church decided they could do it on a Saturday. That Saturday morning, my pastor and I arrived ready for work.

In Kenya there is no ready-mixed cement delivered in large trucks. All of it must be mixed with shovel in hand on the ground. This is an all-day, back-breaking job. About 20 men showed up to work that day. The women of the church met with Tammy and our pastor's wife to make lunch. We finished in the afternoon, completely exhausted.

My pastor and his wife stayed with us for about three weeks. They got to meet and fellowship with the believers of our church. Even to this day, many of our brothers and sisters here speak of them fondly.

It took about five months after my pastor's visit to get the building into a state fitting to hold our meetings, but that time did come. Once the roof was on, we decided to begin holding services on the site.

The church building was still not finished; it would take another six or seven months. There were no benches, no doors, and no windows. It wasn't painted or plastered. There were no Sunday school rooms and no toilets; but at least we could meet there instead of my living room, which had become very overcrowded by this time.

Finally, after about eight months, we completed the building. We dug a well about 48 feet deep (20 feet of this was through solid coral stone). We did the job using only a hammer and chisel. The stone which came from digging the well was used to make the blocks to build the nursery school, saving precious funds for other things. The toilets were completed, and we had slowly been building and adding benches.

Now the church was finished, and we decided to have a celebration of thanksgiving to God for his goodness in giving this church building to the community.

For the celebration, the women all prepared a feast. We had roasted goat meat, Ugali (a paste made from cornmeal), kitheri (corn and beans), and chapatis (fried bread pancake). We sang and praised the Lord and then finished with preaching and prayer. It was a wonderful time. In my mind, I knew this was only half the battle. Now I would need to concentrate fully on establishing the people of this church.

In conclusion, I want the reader to understand this was no overnight building. The work of erecting this building took more than two years and was probably more taxing than any other single phase of the ministry. There were disputes about how to build, what to build, and when to build. Many times I had to play peacemaker when church members disagreed on plans. I played the

62

part of contractor, designer, and laborer. I had to oversee each and every aspect. I had to deal with the pressure of keeping materials available for those doing the work when at times there were no funds to buy anything.

In addition, there were also the daily responsibilities of being the pastor. This involved visiting, praying for, helping the sick, providing transport to hospitals, and guiding people spiritually. Sometimes I would experience anguish at how slowly the work was progressing. I would feel defeated at times when I had hoped to see people attain a certain spiritual level and they did not. My feelings continually got in the way of reality. Yet, in everything, God truly was blessing the work. I learned to keep my faith and trust in Him. My feelings would never be an accurate barometer of the work. Believe me, I know it is not easy to dismiss what one feels. Some people glibly say, "Don't trust your feelings," as if you can take them out of your mind and put them in some darkened corner of a closet somewhere. It's not that easy. It is particularly difficult if you are like me, a very single-minded person, who finds it difficult to concentrate on anything other than the goal which I have placed before myself. I work diligently to achieve my goals. This means that any distraction can bring me great frustration and at times discouragement. This is how I am, but I have learned to temper my frustration by reminding myself of two important truths. The first is, this is God's work not mine. It is the glory of God which is to show forth in this ministry. It is His ability to work in men's hearts which will establish the work. The second truth is, God is in control. He will accomplish His goals, and it is very possible that they may differ from mine.

These two truths may seem too simple, but they are easy to forget when actively engaged in ministry. If one keeps these truths pivotal in his thinking, it will be a great source of help in keeping goals subordinate to God's purpose.

It is only by understanding and reminding myself of these two simple truths, and the grace of God, which have kept me moving forward through many difficult days.

# CHAPTER EIGHT

## - Growth and Stability -

*"And I say also unto thee, That thou art Peter,*

*and upon this rock I will build my church; and*

*the gates of hell shall not prevail against it."*
Matthew 16:18

*"For other foundation can no man lay than*

*that is laid, which is Jesus Christ."*
1 Corinthians 3:11

Another step I felt necessary in establishing the Church spiritually was to provide the Sunday school with a good quality, biblically-sound curriculum. I thought about how I might do this. Basically, I had two choices. I would write my own curriculum or I could use a published curriculum. As I thought about which way to go, I realized that it would take much effort, time, and study to write my own curriculum. In addition, I would have to figure out how to link the lessons together and make them applicable to each age group. On the other hand, a published curriculum would do all this for me. So I decided to use a published curriculum. I wrote to one publisher in the USA which I knew to be doctrinally sound. The publisher in return sent me, free of charge, complete curriculums for each age group. All I had to do was choose the ones applicable to our church's Sunday school, translate and change certain applications to fit Kenyan cultural issues. In using these published curriculums the teachers would have greater resources than I felt I could provide alone.

After obtaining a curriculum, I began a media center in the church. At the outset, one might think a media center in a third world is unnecessary. But I believe it is more necessary here than in churches in developed countries. My reason is this. In countries like the USA, Christian literature, music, and audio tapes are readily available at a fairly reasonable cost. Here, many people do not even own a Bible; and good Christian books and tapes are expensive and scarce. Therefore, I thought if I could collect an array of quality training materials, Christian books, and tapes and make them available to the people of the church, it would contribute much to their spiritual development.

I began by asking Christian people in the USA to help us by contributing books to our library. Some of them did, and we soon had a shelf full of good basic reading resources. Also, some churches had been sending audio tapes to me of their worship services on a regular basis. I decided that instead of keeping these tapes only for occasional listening by me or my family, I would make them available to everyone in the church. So I made a space for these tapes also. Last, I had some old Christian magazines, journals, and Sunday school quarterlies which I added to the library. This became our media center. It is not large. It occupies the top of a table in the back of the church. Anyone can come anytime to read or study within the church, but I do not allow the material to be taken from the property because they may be lost. By encouraging people to study and making these materials available, I believe the people of the church will continue to grow in their understanding and in their abilities to communicate the Bible. One other benefit of the media center is it will provide a good study center for the church's future national pastor.

During the time of establishing the media center, the church formerly opened its nursery school. All children in Kenya who enter primary school must have previously attended a nursery school. Therefore, I determined that a church nursery school could benefit in the establishment and stability of the church. There were several ways in which it could do this. First, it would serve as an evangelistic outreach to the children of the community. Second, it would fill an educational need in the community. Third, it would provide needed revenue to the church.

In the nursery school we installed a teacher whom the church had sent to technical school for 15 months to obtain a teaching certificate. She operates the school and collects all the fees. The school is contributing to the stability of the church, both monetarily and spiritually. It is always a great source of blessing for me to go to the school and see these small children, Christian and Muslim, singing and learning about Jesus along with the alphabet, etc. In this way, I believe the church is reaching into the homes of people who would not be reached by other means.

As time progressed and more people began coming to the services, I determined a church-wide, community-wide meeting would be of benefit to the church. We labeled it a Revival/Crusade meeting. There were to be three services per day for three consecutive days. I hope that God might be pleased to accomplish several tasks in the meetings.

Basically, the tasks I hoped to see accomplished were these:

1- It would be a time for the believers to evaluate their lives.
2- They would receive instruction for practical Christian living.
3- They would develop strong relationships and a sense of Christian family one with the other.
4- They would develop in private prayer and spirituality.
5- They would be strengthened in their faith.
6- They might develop a sense of unity and purpose.
7- They would sense the need to evangelize.
8- The unsaved might come to receive Christ.

The crusade went well and had good attendance. On the last night, at the end of the service, many people did not wish to leave. They continued the service until 6:00 am -- singing, praying, and praising God. I followed up the crusade by preaching a series of messages on evangelism, and we have seen some fruit. I am very thankful to the Lord for blessing these efforts and I am fully aware that without His help, all our work and ideas are vain. Therefore, each effort was bathed in prayer for God's help and blessing.

With the need for spiritual development, I was also aware of the need to develop the church as an independent, self-functioning organization. It must be able to govern and support itself. It must be able to carry out the business of the ministry.

To me this seemed to be the greatest challenge. Most people here are poor compared to the average American. Most usually do not plan ahead. They live day by day. If money is obtained, it is used with no thought of what they will do tomorrow. But a church will not succeed functioning like this. It must think about things such as paying its expenses, paying the pastor, and being accountable for what has been given. A church must be a good example and steward as it is recognized as a house of God.

I realized that a program of order must be established if the church would ever be able to function as an organization. The first step in establishing order was to establish recognized leaders. To do this, I recommended one of the men to serve as a deacon. I explained the office of deacon to the church in a series of teaching sessions, and then this brother was voted in as our first deacon. Since that time we have installed another deacon and are planning to install one more as this is being written. The deacons have done remarkably well in serving the church.

Once the first deacon was installed, we began holding formal business meetings with treasurers and secretaries being elected. People have begun to understand that they must make decisions for the church. Not one, not some, but all of them together bear the responsibility.

Second, we drafted a church covenant which was voted on and signed by each church member. This covenant is given to each prospective church member to be read and signed before he/she joins the church.

Concerning offerings, the deacons and the pastor determine the prospective budget, and it is brought before the church for approval. Revisions are made to the budget as needed.

The most difficult of all the tasks has been determining the pastor. Yet, this is essential as he will be the primary leader and mover of the church.

There were a few men in the church whom I had begun to look at as prospective pastors. One was named Paulo, Paulo was tall, handsome, and well groomed. He had a pleasant sounding, deep voice and a distinguished manner about him. I thought, "This man has great potential." He had been saved and baptized in our church, he was well educated, and his family lived with him. In Kenya many husbands live far away from their wives and children because of work.

Paulo was studying in our institute, and I believed he would make a great pastor. I made him my assistant and began training him with that purpose in mind. He progressed wonderfully and seemed to be an answer to prayer.

After about two months, I asked him about becoming pastor of the church. He expressed his agreement and affirmed his belief that God was calling him to do this. I began working with Paulo three days per week. Together we studied doctrine, hermeneutics, and practices. I took him with me on my weekly visits to the nursery school. In these visits, I would discuss areas of improvement and receive the students' fees to be deposited in the church's account. I wanted Paulo to understand each detail of the ministry. He caught on quickly and after about six months, I was ready to bring him before the church to be voted on as the new pastor. Although I was delighted with Paulo, I continued to pray and ask God to guide in this matter and to prevent him from becoming Pastor if he was not the right man.

One afternoon, two weeks before I was going to bring Paulo before the church, he came to my house. During this visit, he informed me that he had been offered an opportunity to go to England and study computers. He had decided to accept the opportunity.

Needless to say, I was very disappointed. All the months I had put into preparing him as pastor. The help I had extended to him and the confidence I had put in his call, all seemed to disappear during that conversation. Nevertheless, I also felt a sense of gratitude. I had asked God to show me if this man was not the right one, and He did so.

With Paulo out of the picture, I turned my focus toward other possible candidates. Another young man whom I considered earlier came to mind. His name was Joseph. Joseph had come to the church about three years earlier. He was saved, but not in our church. He had a good knowledge of the Bible because he had taken various correspondence courses. He was shorter than Paulo with a soft-spoken, mild-tempered manner about him.

Originally, I had dismissed Joseph as a candidate for one reason, his wife. Although she was a Christian, she did not live with him. It was not because of a bad marriage. They were happily married. It was because of his work. Joseph was in town to work, but his wife needed to stay at their homeplace. In that way, she could farm their land while he earned money on a job. I believed that a good pastor must have his family with him. So I didn't even ask if he would be willing to bring her to stay with him if he were the pastor. I simply dismissed him from my consideration. But now God had brought him back into my thoughts.

Understanding that sometimes the nationals find it difficult to be completely straightforward with the missionary, I asked for our first deacon, Shadrach Ngala, to speak with Joseph about bringing his wife to Mtwapa and becoming the pastor of the church.

Shadrach had been a great help to me both personally and in the establishment of the church. He is a respected man in the community and understands how we Westerners think. I knew I could depend on him to get Joseph's true feelings on this very important matter.

Within a few days, Shadrach brought me the results of the meeting with Joseph. It seems that Joseph had always felt that God was calling him to be the pastor, but he didn't know how to tell anyone. Shadrach told Joseph of the need have his wife living with him if he were to be the pastor. Joseph was very straightforward with Shadrach and informed him that his wife was at home because by farming she was able to help provide for their debts, etc. He stated that he was willing to bring her here, but the expenses would be too much for him to bear.

Shadrach then explained how the church would help meet his expenses. The two of them figured out the minimum amount which the church would need to provide Joseph's sustenance. As pastor, he would not need to pay rent because at the time of building, we built a three-room apartment on the back of the church to serve as the future pastor's residence. He would not need to buy water because we had dug a well on the property. Therefore, they figured he would only need to buy clothes, food, and pay school fees in the event his wife and he were able to have children. The total amount they figure he would need would be about 2,000/= shillings per month (about $45.00). Shadrach presented me with the figure, and I agreed that it was reasonable. We met with the other deacons and the other leaders of the church and agreed that if, and when, this amount not be met with the weekly offerings and nursery school fees, the church would take up a special offering to make up the difference.

Everyone seemed to agree that Joseph was the right man, and he will be installed as pastor before my departure from Kenya for a furlough in about four months. The church has managed to save a good portion of their offerings to provide for Joseph in case of lean months.

The nursery school is up and running. Each Sunday, the Sunday school teachers take their classes, offerings are taken and counted, Children's church operates and special singers sing. Basically, there are people in place to operate the church. At this time, it is between 95-99% self-supporting, and I see no reason that it will not continue so after my departure.

It has been six years since we first arrived in Kenya. There have been many struggles to overcome. We have called this strange land with its people and their unusual ways "home." They have been our friends and we theirs.

There were defeats and there were victories. We have seen God completely change behaviors and attitudes by the gospel. We have seen what some said was impossible become possible. A truly indigenous church has basically been planted. It is not because of us as missionaries, but by the power of the Spirit and faith in God's promise that "...*the gates of Hell shall not prevail against.*" Glory to His Wonderful name!

# CHAPTER NINE

## - Everyday Life -

*"And He said unto them, Take heed,*

*and beware of covetousness:*

*for a man's life consisteth not*

*in the abundance of the things*

*which he possesseth. "*

Luke 12:15

People are always curious about life on the mission field. So, in this chapter, I will attempt to give some insight into our everyday life.

Let me begin by discussing life at home. Since most home life revolves around the kitchen, I will tell you about food. It may surprise some to hear that "monkey brains" is not on our regular menu. For the most part, we eat the same kinds of things as we do in America, with the exception of prepared and packaged foods.

Most everything is sold fresh. There are very little canned or frozen foods, and those that do exist are very expensive. We have learned to live without things like Frito's and TV dinners. Occasionally we get a package from the USA in which some wonderful person has put Fruit Loops and Lay's potato chips. This usually brings squeals of excitement and anticipation from the girls and me. Occasionally I have dreams of McDonald's "Big Macs" or "Kentucky Fried Chicken," but usually I'm able to restrain myself and not gobble up the bedpost.

In addition to the unavailability of American snack food, packaged instant foods and mixes are also unavailable -- things like instant pudding, cake mixes, bread mixes, dressing mixes, packaged sauces and gravies. This means that almost everything must be prepared from scratch. Therefore, if you are a fan of frozen french fries, prepare to suffer.

Going shopping is also a unique experience. We live about thirty minutes from town. The drive to town is hot and the road is embedded with pot holes. By the time of your arrival, you are usually, as Elvis Presley put it, "all shook up!"

In Mombasa there are no shopping malls or true department stores. Therefore, if you want clothes, you must go to the clothes store; if you want hardware, you go to the hardware store; if you need a light bulb, to the electricity shop. In most cases, if you go to town needing ten items, you probably will need to visit eight different shops or more to find them, and the shops may not be close together.

Town itself is very crowded and most of your time walking from shop to shop is spent guarding your wallet, dodging beggars, and telling guides that you are not a tourist and do not need their assistance. If you need to get vegetables, there is a large open-air market in town. Most of the vegetables are sold in open-air markets of this kind or smaller. You should carry your own bag to put the vegetables in and don't allow anyone to carry it for you, or else your helper and the "veggies" may disappear after you have paid the bill. Remember, too, keep everything with you and don't put it into your car until you are ready to go. Our car has been broken into six times as a result of this. As you can probably tell, I have a great dislike for town, but it is a necessary evil. Thankfully, we only need to go about once per week.

Another aspect of life here is shortages. Sometimes, but not often, there are shortages of foods like bread, milk, and sugar. But there are two shortages you can always depend on. They are water and electricity. If it were not for the fact that we have a well, we would literally never have water in our house. God has been so good in providing us with this great advantage over many others here. Electricity is another problem. One can usually depend on the electricity to go out at least once per week for a few hours. Even when there is electricity, it fluctuates. At night you can watch the lights go up and down, which plays havoc with electric appliances.

I feel it important to tell you that I am not complaining about these things. I understand it is by God's grace that we enjoy the benefits of electricity and other things which we have and I am truly thankful. This is only to give you a picture of life here, but please do not think I am writing with an ungrateful heart. You need to see that shortages are part of the routine. As one old Italian man who lived here for many years put it, "This is Africa, and in Africa, there is aplenty of onea thinga. That onea thinga isa shortages."

Concerning our family and social life, it is limited. There are not many days during the year when we get to socialize as we did in America. In America, we could go out to dinner with friends or have them over to our house and play games.  Here it is very difficult to do so, mainly because most of the people we're working with cannot afford to go out to eat, and to come to our house is difficult because of the distance to walk.  It is also difficult because of the vast cultural differences.  We do socialize some, but it is very different from when friends came over in the states.  I'm not saying it is bad, but we do get homesick for "American fellowship" from time to time.

Our three daughters are home-schooled. Sometimes we worry about their lack of socialization with other young people, but they seem to handle it very well.  Every year they take the Iowa Skills Achievement test and score in the top 10% of students in the USA for their grade levels.  Tammy teaches them Monday through Friday, an average of six hours each day.  Preparation, teaching, and recordkeeping , along with her other duties as a wife, mother, and the ministry, keep her extremely busy.  Sometimes, I don't think people realize how much a missionary's wife has to do.  I am grateful for my wife and her willingness in doing this work.

We also have two Indian friends named Tobia and Fatuma.  We met them about three years ago.  Tobia is an up-and-coming business man who seems to be prospering well.   He is good looking with a short beard and mustache.   He likes to joke and laugh, and he is very pleasant company.   Fautma is a beautiful young woman with long black hair, olive skin, and dark brown eyes.

Her personality is as pleasant as her husband's, and we enjoy the times we are able to visit together. They have three children near to ours in ages, and they all are best of friends. This has been a particular blessing for us, as we felt the girls needed some good playmates with whom they could relate.

In the church we have made many friends. One is called Mama Joyce. She is a high school teacher, and she has four children which she is raising alone. Her daughter and my oldest daughter, Lucinda, are best friends. They enjoy sharing books and just spending time talking together. Joyce's husband abandoned her long ago when the children were young. She is a wonderful Christian woman and very industrious. When we visit with her, we usually spend the time singing African hymns, eating, and praying.

Another friend is Shadrach Ngala. Shadrach was the first deacon in the church. He is my best friend of all the others in the church. He is intelligent, industrious, and a true leader in the community. He has given me level-headed advice on many issues.

There are so many in the church that I can't name them all, and we love each of them and enjoy our fellowship together; but it is still not the same as the fellowship we get in the states and we don't expect it to be.

There are some things which are a constant aggravation to us. One is beggars and people you don't know always coming to your home or to you on the street asking for handouts. If it's not the beggars, then there are conmen trying to trick you out of money. Next, having to get in the car at any hour of the day or night to take someone to the doctor or hospital, or they need some kind of help. They need a doctor, the house fell down, no money for rent, no money for food, school fees, etc., etc., etc.

Now don't think I am some kind of Ebeneezer Scrooge character, but all these things happen fairly regular. Many times these needs are not nearly as serious as a person wants you to believe they are. Therefore, one must be careful that he doesn't become known as "Mr. Charity" or else he will have no money to minister or to help when someone has a real need, or even to pay his own expenses.

When true needs do arise, the people know I will help; but they have also learned I am no pushover. There are many instances when I have helped in true times of need. I remember one morning at about 2:00 am, I was awakened from sleep. Outside the house was an old man whom I recognized. He shouted excitedly, "kuja sasa, Mtoto amekuja, damu sana!!!" (come immediately, the baby has come, there is a lot of blood!!!) I knew this old man, but I couldn't figure out what he was talking about. I knew from the intensity of his speech something must

83

be terribly wrong. I ran to my closet and hurriedly got dressed. I grabbed the keys to the pumpkin (our van), unlocked it, and got in with the old man beside me. He began directing me to the place that was the subject of his excitement. We started out on the hard surface road and went until it ran into a dirt road. After traveling quite a distance, he directed me to take a right. "But there is no road there!" I exclaimed. "Endelea, njia iko hii!" (Continue, this is the way to go), he said frantically. I turned to the right and headed into the bush. As we traveled deeper and deeper into the darkened forest, a fear began to grip me. What if this was a trick? What if he was taking me out into this bush to be robbed or worse? What if he was getting me away from my family so that thieves could rob our house? I knew this old man, but not very well. As the van bumped along through the forest I prayed silently, "Lord, I don't know where I am going. I am not even sure why I am going there. All I know is there seems to be a major emergency and my help is needed. I ask you Lord, please guide and protect me from any possible. harm. Please guard my family at home from anything or anyone who might try to harm them. In Jesus name, Amen." I had to trust God!

After a few more minutes we came to a clearing, and I could see the kerosene lanterns of a small village. Standing outside of one small hut must have been 25-30 women. They were all wailing and screaming in their mother tongue. The old man directed me to the hut. I pulled the van up in front of the door of the house, got out, and hurried inside. Never before in my entire life had I seen such a sight. A young African woman lay on the dirt floor in a pool of blood. She was barely conscious and unbelievably pale. In a darkened corner of the room lay a newborn baby. It was dead. I knew that if we did not get this girl to the hospital soon she would die also. I quickly called for some of the men in the village to get the girl up and put her into my car. The old man and two women climbed in the car to accompany her. I started the car and we sped off for the hospital. I don't know how I managed to get out of those woods, but it was in half the time it took me to get there.

The hospital was about 20 minutes away. As I drove, I prayed that God would help us make it in time. When we arrived at the hospital, they took her in immediately and started blood transfusions. The doctor in charge told me that I had literally saved this woman's life. Another 15 or 20 minutes and she would have bled to death.

After making sure the girl was being taken care of, I drove the old man and two women back to my house. It was about 5:00 am. They informed me they needed to go and bury the baby. "Right now?" I asked. "Yes, it our custom," they said. It seems that among this tribe if a young baby dies, it must be buried immediately in the dirt floor of its parents' house.

They quickly left to do this, and I went in the house to share my experience of the night with Tammy. We went to our bedroom and bowed our heads to thank God for His protection and help. Then I went out and washed the blood from the interior of my car.

Later, I learned the reason for the problem was the baby was being born feet first and was not coming out. So, the women attending the birth decided to grab the feet of the baby and pull him out. Of course this resulted in serious problems.

For about three months after that episode, I would wake up to find a bag of corn at my gate almost every day. This was that family's way of thanking me.

There have been numerous episodes of helping people in emergencies such as this. When I came here I didn't know part of a missionary's duties would be as an ambulance driver.

One of the great joys we have as a family is getting mail from home. Sometimes you feel a bit lonely and homesick. When a letter comes, it will change your whole attitude. I only wish folks in America understood how much joy a letter or card can bring.

The most dreadful thing for any missionary is to hear the news of the death of a loved one back home. This happened to me on two occasions.

The first was when I got news that my mother was dying of cancer. I was on the field, but I was in a position to be able to go home and minister to her and my family. This I did and I will be forever grateful to God for allowing me to do so.

The second occasion came just five months before I was to go home on furlough. It was just before Christmas when I received a telephone call from my sister-in-law informing me that my grandmother was in the hospital and it "did not look good."

My grandmother was a great lady who had worked hard most of her life. She supported her own family and together with my mother, raised me and my brother. For several years she struggled with crippling arthritis and was completely bedridden. She deserved a rest.

I got the news from my pastor that she had died. I had tried to call my family to find out about her condition but could get no answer, so I phoned the pastor. He reluctantly informed me of my grandmother's death. I was deeply saddened. I wanted very much to go home. I wanted to be with my other family members to offer help and support. I wanted to see my grandma's face one last time. But I couldn't do it. I was not at position to leave this time. I did not have the finances, and the church was at a critical stage of its development. I wanted to drop everything and go home, but that was impossible.

I loved my grandmother dearly, but my going home could not help her now. Perhaps I might have been able to help the survivors in our family; who knows? I felt helpless and guilty for not being at home during that time. I called my family members and attempted to offer words of encouragement, but this did not seem to be nearly enough. God was giving me grace. I just wanted to be sure my loved ones were doing all right also.

Since then, I have spoken with other missionaries and learned that this is a common concern for each of them. Times like this never will be easy. There will always be the dilemma of whether to go home or to stay. We just have to lean on God's divine sovereignty during these circumstances.

So what is everyday life like in Kenya? It is boring, exciting, difficult, and wonderful. It's like no other place. Here you can be in town and experience the marvels of modern civilization, or you can go 20 minutes into the bush and witness how people lived long ago and still do. Yes, indeed, we have missed some things, but we have had advantages and opportunities we could never have had in the states. We have seen many of the marvels and wonders of God's creation here. The animals, the land, the people, and so much more. Truly there is nothing better than serving Jesus Christ. After all, it doesn't really matter where you hang your hat because He is the one who grants abundant life. Amen!

# CHAPTER TEN

## - Tales of Adventure -

*"In the Lord I put my trust:*

*how say ye to my soul,*

*flee as a bird to your mountain?"*

Psalm 11:1

I have always enjoyed tales of adventure. I love reading stories about the early pioneers and how they persevered in the New World, or swashbuckling pirates on the high seas. I believe this is one reason I have always been interested in mission. Tales of men like David Livingstone or David Brainard, as they endured danger and hardship in order to carry God's message of hope to people, have always allured me. Therefore, if you are like me, this chapter is for you!

I suppose every missionary has a few tales of adventure. Probably this is more true of those who serve in the developing world than those in industrialized lands. In this chapter, I will share some of mine.

Before beginning, I want you to realize that these are not everyday occurrences. They are separated by months and years. So don't get the wrong impression.

One of the first things to happen to our family was when we were returning home from a trip to Nairobi. The trip from Nairobi to Mombasa is several hours long. The road is usually in poor condition with many deep pot holes and erosion eating away at its sides. In addition, it runs mostly through wilderness with the exception of a few tiny bush towns. There are three main stops where you can purchase fuel: "Hunters Lodge:, about two and a half hours from Nairobi; "Mtito Endei:, another hour from Hunter's Lodge; and "Voi", about three hours from

Mtito Endei. In between these stops one must pray that he doesn't have car trouble.

On this particular trip, we had left Nairobi and been driving for about two hours when suddenly the fan belt broke off from the engine. Since my Volkswagen had an air-cooled engine, I realized I needed to stop immediately to replace the belt or risk serious engine damage. I pulled the car off the road and shut off the engine. I got my tool box out from under my seat where it was stored and proceeded to the rear of the vehicle to repair the belt. My daughters stayed in the car and Tammy got out with me in case I needed her assistance.

Suddenly one of the girls shouted back to us, "Look, there's some monkeys in the road!" Sure enough, as I looked ahead, I saw a troop of about 20-30 baboons coming down the road towards our car. The nearer these animals came to us, the more concerned I became.

There were reasons for my concern. The baboons along this stretch of road have no fear of humans. We have heard horror stories from locals of how women working their garden would lay their babies nearby to nap on the ground and the baboons would come and take them. On another occasion, an Asian friend of mine, after his car broke down on the road, had them peel the rubber from the windshield of his car in an attempt to gain entrance to the vehicle. We had been warned that these animals could be quite "Kali" (mean), so beware.

Realizing that these animals were interested in us, I told Tammy to get in the car and lock the doors. I hurriedly continued to get the belt replaced. Within seconds, the baboons were upon us. They completely surrounded the vehicle. One particularly large one, which must have been the leader, came and sat uncomfortably close to me as I worked on the engine. I looked at his large head. It had a gray/white stripe running down the center. On his face was a kind of sinister grin, and I could see his long sharp canine teeth. If this was his attempt to intimidate me, it was working very well. My hands were trembling, causing me difficulty in finishing the repairs. The baboon began inching his way closer and closer to me until he was about an arm's length away. I thought, "What am I going to do? He could be upon me in half a second if he chose to." I definitely did not want to challenge him in any way, as I knew I would be no match for him; but I also didn't want him to come any closer. I looked down into my tool box to see if there was anything I could use to defend myself in case he decided to jump me. In the bottom of the tool box there was a large pipe wrench. I took it in my hand and extended my arm fully so that the wrench was now aimed in front of the baboon's face. I began to wave the wrench in an up-and-down motion, hoping that this would intimidate him enough to keep him away. With my other hand, I tightened the slack on the belt, which I had managed to get attached by this time.

Once the belt was tightened, I closed the lid to the engine compartment and slowly got in the car. A feeling of great relief came over me as I shut the door, realizing that we could now get away from these creatures.

I put the key in the ignition and turned it, but there was no start. I tried again, no start. The battery was dead. "Oh no!" I thought, "What do I do now?" Usually there would have been a car or truck to pass us by this time, but none were in sight. The baboons were all around us, but they had not attempted to get in the car yet. I knew that if something didn't happen soon their curiosity would overcome them and they would begin to try in earnest to break in. In desperation, I put my head down on the steering wheel and prayed, "Lord, please help us!" At that very instant over the horizon came a huge bus full of people. As it came near to us it stopped, the driver pulled on the air horn. The extremely loud noise caused the baboons to scatter off into the bush. The driver, accompanied by a couple of passengers, got off the bus and said, "Got trouble?" "Sure do," I answered while praising God in my mind. I informed the driver of our dead battery. He told me to get in the car and they would push it to see if it would jump start. We did and it did start. I thanked the driver and we were off with no more trouble the rest of the way home. I should have prayed earlier. It might have saved a lot of anxiety.

When we returned home, we all laughed about the sight of my waving that wrench in front of that baboon's face. I told my family, "That's one of the uses for a pipe wrench."

"What?" asked my wife.

"Yea," I said, "that's how it came to be known as a `monkey wrench'."

We have also had adventures with other creatures from the wild. For a while my wife was raising chickens. We noticed that they began disappearing. Our yard worker informed us that he believed it was a snake.

One afternoon we were all sitting in the living room when our yard worker and the neighbor's yard worker began yelling very loudly out in the garden. We ran out to see what the commotion was about. There in the garden they had cornered a four-foot long cobra. It was coiled in a striking position. One worker kept its attention while the other came up behind it with a machete and cut off its head. What a relief to be rid of that thing!

On another occasion, one morning Tammy got up to fix breakfast while I continued to sleep. After preparing breakfast she came into the bedroom to wake me up. Suddenly, she let out a loud scream which woke me instantly.

"What's the matter with you?" I said, still flat on my back in bed.

"It's a snake!" she screamed.

"Where? I don't see anything," I said.

"Look right above you!" she said.

I looked through my sleepy eyes and there hanging directly over my head was a green mamba. The green mamba is very deadly. It is one of the most poisonous snakes in the world. Apparently it had come in through the window at the  head of our bed in pursuit of a small lizard on the curtain. Slowly and carefully, I slid out of the bed onto the floor trying not to attract the snake's attention away from the lizard on our curtain.

Once safely out of the bed, I went and got a machete. I went to the outside of the window and began to shake the window hoping to draw the snake's attention. I succeeded and it came rushing out toward me. As it did, I quickly shut the window, trapping it's body. Then I proceeded to shop off its head. Up until that time, we did not have screens on the windows. Needless to say, by the next day every window had a screen on it.

Kenya is famous for its wonderful wildlife and its game parks. We have been privileged to visit some of them. We have also been chased in these parks by elephant, rhino, and buffalo. One time we were with Tammy's mother and father who were visiting from the

States when a mama elephant with her baby charged at our vehicle. I believe that was a time Tammy's mom will never forget.

Another time when we lived in Likoni, I had to make a trip to Nairobi alone. Tammy and the girls would remain at home. Tammy was doing her housework when our yard worker shouted to her, "Mama, close the door!" Tammy jumped up just in time to see a man running up the steps toward the door. He looked like some kind of wild man. His hair was matted, several teeth were missing, and his clothes were dirty and torn.

This same man had been outside our compound under our dining room window for several days begging for money or food before I had left for Nairobi. I could tell he was probably insane and I knew he was a nuisance; but I figured he was harmless. Before I left for Nairobi, I gave him some money and sent him on his way, never thinking he would try anything.

Yet now this same man had knocked down our yard worker and was running up the stairs to enter the house. Just before he reached the door, Tammy managed to slam and lock it in his face. He pounded on the door for a long time demanding to be let in. Tammy begged him to go and leave her alone. The girls locked themselves in their room. Finally, after some time, she threatened him with the police and he gave up and left. When I arrived back home and heard the story, I was shocked. Thank the Lord no one had been hurt. We never saw that man again.

The last story I want to share with you involves an accident I had. One of the problems here is a shortage of water. God has blessed us with a well, so we have water; but the problem we had was that in the bottom of the well was an old electric pump. The pump was continually breaking down. Therefore, I would have to go down into the well almost every week to repair and re-prime the pump. The way I would do this was to get a strong nylon rope, tie one end to my car, and the other end to my waist. I would put the rope through a pulley mounted on a steel bar which was mounted on large wooden posts on either side of the well. I would hang from the rope and pulley, and Tammy would drive the car forward to lower me into the well and reverse to pull me out. I also had another rope tied to one of the posts as backup. In case my rope broke, I could grab hold of the other.

I had done this same procedure of going in and out of the well many times over several months. It was my only choice as I did not have sufficient funds to buy a new pump.

On one particular day, the pump broke down again. It was during the rainy season, so the ground was quite wet. I went out just as I had done many times before and prepared to enter the well.

What I didn't know was that the rains had caused the bottom of the two posts which were planted in the ground to rot. I got up on the well, slid off the side, and hung suspended 60 feet from the bottom. Tammy was in the car prepared to lower me. As I hung there, I realized I had left my tool pouch on the ground. I shouted for the yard worker to get it for me. As he reached down to get my tools, I suddenly heard a loud pop. One of the posts had broken, the pulley fell and jammed against both ropes, cutting them instantly. I plunged the entire 60 feet, crashing into the pump and iron platform at the bottom, ripping it from the wall. As I was falling, at first I thought I would die. Then a peace came over me. I did not hear any voice or anything like that, but I knew I would be all right. Just before crashing at the bottom, it felt as if something or someone grabbed hold and slowed my fall. I felt absolutely no pain as I hit all that metal.

As I stood up out of the water, I could hear Tammy screaming at the top, "Tony, are you all right? Please answer me!" I told her I was okay and then overwhelmed, I repeatedly began to thank the Lord for my deliverance. Over and over for about three minutes, all I could say was, "Thank you, Jesus."

I was sure I was in a state of shock because I then fished the pump out of the water to put it back on its platform. Upon getting the pump up, I realized the platform had gone. I tied the pump with the small piece of rope that was still around my waist (the rest of it stayed at the top of the well) and hung it on a small protruding piece of iron which remained in the wall.

Soon after that I began to feel a terrible pain in my legs and they began to tremble violently. I told Tammy to get a chair, tie the rope to it and send it down because I could no longer stand up. She lowered the chair and I sat down in the three-foot pool of water. Upon sitting, I lifted my feet out of the water for the first time. Both of my shoes had been knocked off from the impact, and my feet were bent and swollen to the size of large shoe boxes.

Soon, people from the area began arriving after hearing Tammy's screams. Some of them took Tammy into the house as the rest lowered the rope to pull me out.

I refused to allow them to pull me up. I had fallen one time, I didn't treasure the idea of doing it again. The men, knowing that I was not going to be cooperative, talked me into putting the rope around me and telling me they would wait until I was ready. They tricked me. As soon as the rope was around my waist, they began pulling me out in spite of my protest. I realize now they had to do it that way because I would have never given permission.

Once I was out of the well, Tammy rushed me to the hospital. I had injured my left knee, broken every bone in my left foot and ankle, and broken several bones in my right foot. Both feet were a bluish-black color from internal bleeding, and there was extensive tissue damage. I had to have surgery on my left foot and knew, and I would be unable to walk for several weeks. For three months I needed a cane, but today I am okay. My walk is almost normal and I thank God for sparing my life. Oh yeah, my home church bought us a new pump! No more problems! Hallelujah!

There are more stories I could tell, but I think you get the picture. Things are going to happen. This may happen at home or on the mission field. We can't know what adventures lie ahead for us, but we do know the One who is able to keep us through every trial or adventure. God bless you! Pray for us!

# CHAPTER ELEVEN

## - Summing It All Up -

The main objective of this book is to show mission life in practice. It is not about a great hero of the faith; most assuredly it is not about that. It is about ordinary people called by God to do a work.

The work is to preach the gospel of Jesus Christ, to proclaim God's truth, and His will in salvation. It is being a witness.

It involves steadfastness, a spirit of perseverance, and a zeal which will overcome obstacles. A faith that is sure when circumstances change. It is about a true motive which puts God's glory and purpose above all else.

A missionary is a developer of people. He trains workers and spiritual leaders to serve in local churches. He plants and establishes those churches. He is one who follows God's lead wherever that may be. He trusts God for provision and protection in that leading.

These things do not mean that he is superhuman, for certainly he is not. There are times when he doubts God's will. There are times when he is confused and does not know God's perfect will. Sometimes he is afraid; other times he may seem bold. What is he? He is a missionary. Just a person who is trusting in the power of God to provide a harvest.

"Did we in our own strength confide
Our striving would be losing,
Were not the right man on our side,
The man of God's own choosing.
Dost ask who that may be?
Christ Jesus, it is He.
Lord Sabaoth is His name
From age to age the same...
And He must win the battle!"

--Martin Luther

Amen!!

The little plywood hut from which we were chased.

Our living room had gotten very crowded.

The plot and first load of blocks.

The slab is poured.

105

Once the roof was on, we began to hold meetings.

The well was dug using a chisel and hammer.

There was still some work to do.

Tony and his two deacons.

Simon at work.

From left to right:  Joseph, James, and Amos.

Tammy's parents with church members after church.

The Crusade went well.

**Baraka and Tony**

**Tony & Joseph**

A place of our own!

The Giriama tribe sing a special during the Crusade.

Joseph, Daniel (with a smile), and Tony

The Ngalla Family

111

Our house in Likoni.

Our house in Mtwapa.

School at home.

This green mamba hung directly over my head.

Jessica holding the cobra we killed in our yard.

113

Lucinda with Elizabeth.

Using your head in Africa.

114

Likoni ferry.

The pumpkin.

I fell all the way to the bottom of this well.

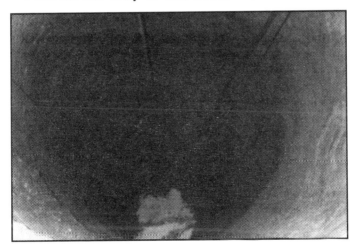

ON

SAFARI

IN

KENYA

116